The Life Of Fly

The Life Of Fly

Magnus Muhr

CHRONICLE BOOKS

SAN FRANCISCO

First published in the United States in 2011
by Chronicle Books, LLC.

First Published in the United Kingdom in 2010
by Summersdale Publishers Ltd.

Copyright © 2010 by Magnus Muhr

Library of Congress Cataloging-in-Publication
Data is available.

ISBN: 978-0-8118-7906-4

Manufactured in China

10 9 8 7 6 5 4 3 2 1

Chronicle Books LLC
680 Second Street
San Francisco, CA 94107
www.chroniclebooks.com

no flies were harmed in the making of this book.

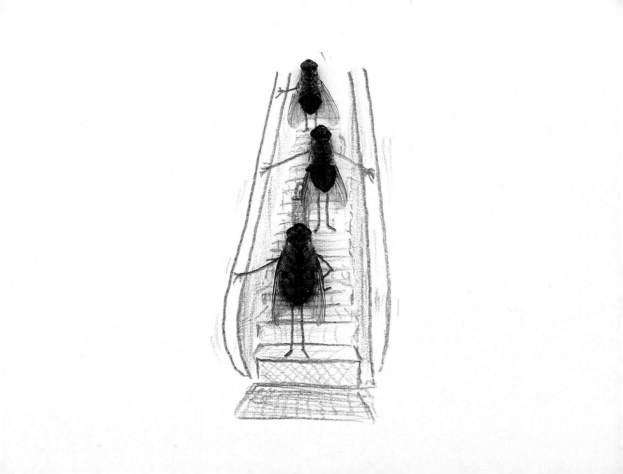

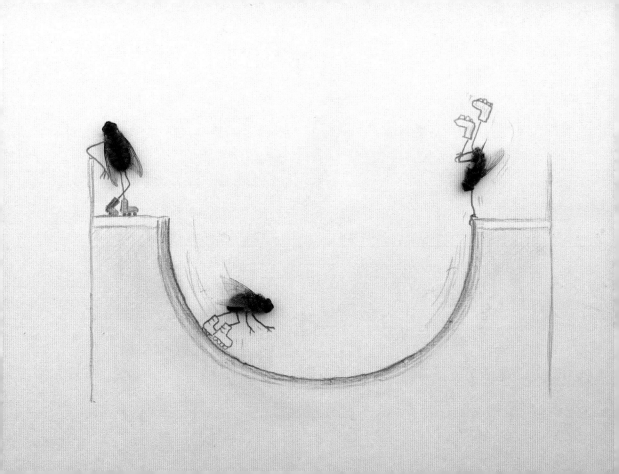

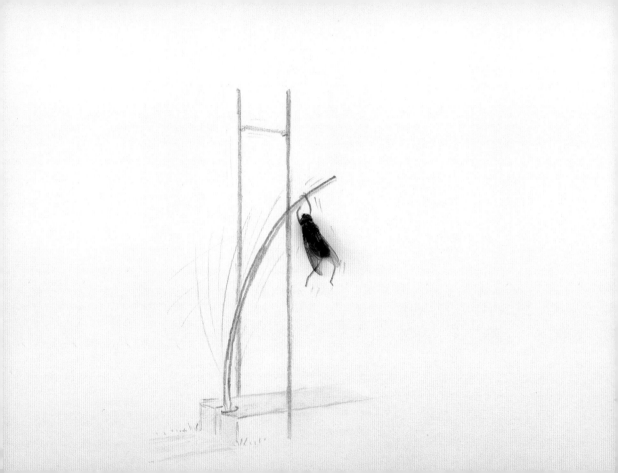

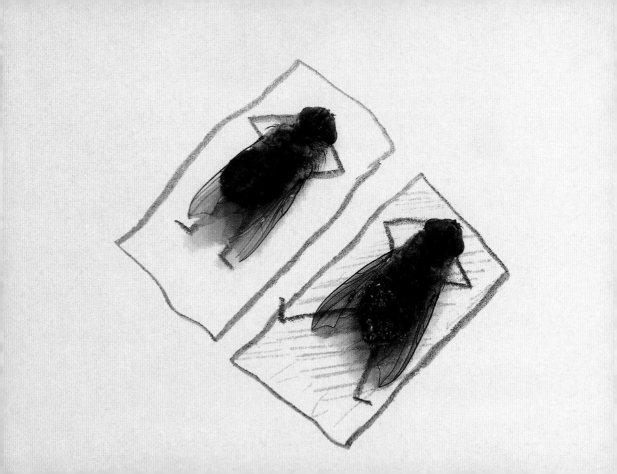

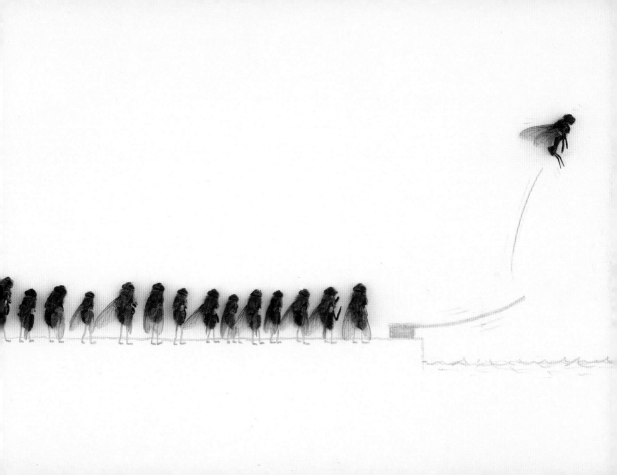

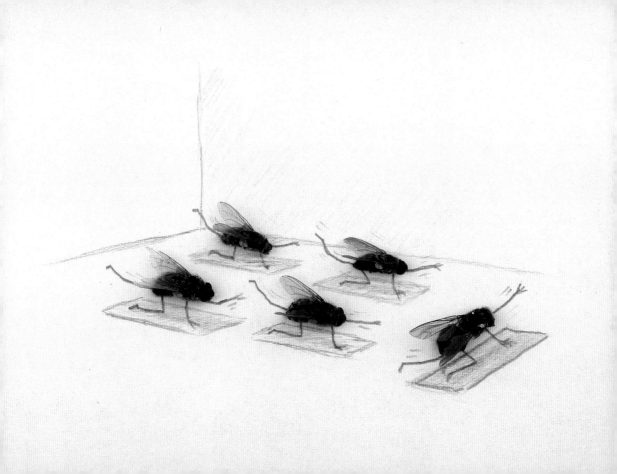

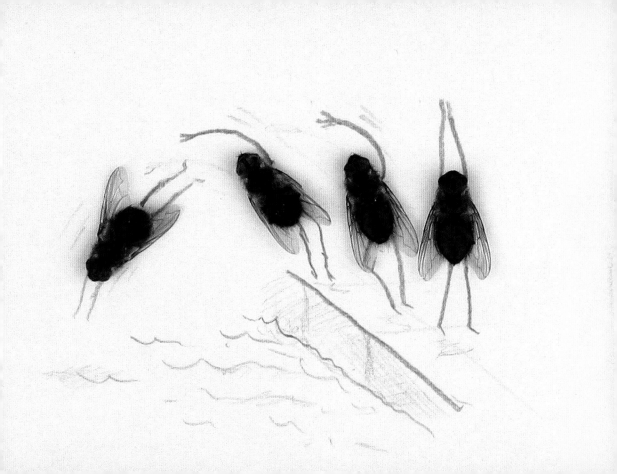

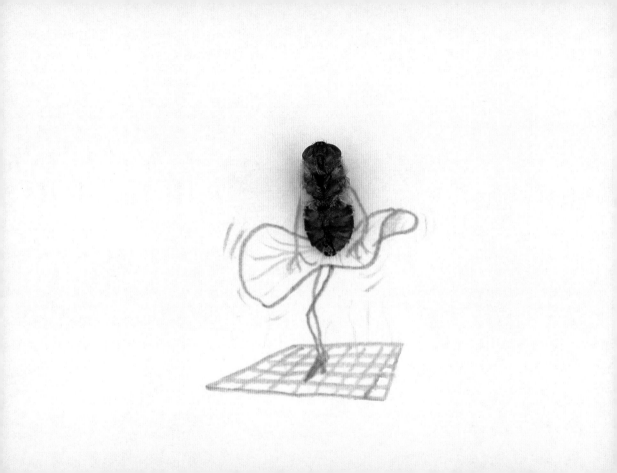

THE END

ABOUT the AUThOr

**Magnus Muhr is an avid photographer, with
nature, portraits, and nudes as his favorite fields.
He lives in Sweden.**